I0202492

LETTING THE SEASONS

POEMS

NANCY DAVIES

Published by Nouveau Proletariat Press
nouveauproletariat.com

ISBN-13: 978-0692068144

Also by Nancy Davies

The People Decide: Oaxaca's Popular Assembly
Tourists to the Rebellion
Messages in a Small Town

LETTING THE SEASONS

Contents

Letting The Seasons

PART ONE

Letting The Seasons

THE EXPEDITION

We hurtle down roads in search of the rig
veda—scrawled on wet cement in front of the first temple ever?
On sand-hills metal mantises pray
for oil, a rocking repeat of shawled men at the
wailing wall. Wind-rigs go round, snickering
memories of birds in Iowa: whatbird,
whatbird, whatbird?

Hymn of the absolute, inscribed with imperishable
alphabets. In the beginning God taught school.
Little devas jammed pens in an inkpot,
Rorschached creation. They dipped the braid
of our soil-colored camp-cook. At night
her hair grows knots like a mulberry. The moon's
face in a gothic tower ticks back
sloughing centuries in search of gold
soda-pop, horses, cattle, male off-spring.

Winds gather, jackals loose at the bones
of our site. Timber slithers between their teeth.
The dig struggles in ropes of rain, snaring
beetles and lizards larger than rodents.
By dusk two pick-ups on a mound remain
with us perched on their hoods, while new rivers
wash huts with dry records; tents creep
away. Who were the twins who passed here at dawn
fetching rice in a bundle? Their dark limbs
return words they forgot to deliver.

Mud, though not civilized, twitches.
In our boots, in our hair, in our shovels it shivers
with fever. Silver combs come knock at our knees,
begging forgiveness. Not what I want. I want
to read sanskrit hammered on rock: "We drank soma
and fought. We have wanted to tell you
for a long time how we died."

The Wall

After the rain we went to look—
astonished and dismayed. How can rock decay?
There the crushed disarray
of our neighbor's rhododendron bushes,
and the stones heavy where they lay
seemed ultimate and new—never again
will things stand quite that way.

The old man raged over his garden,
clearly ruined, leaves ripped,
stems bent and stripped.
Above earth-bones gaped
like a face from which flesh had slipped.
The jagged edge wept body fluids,
mud or plasma—while we watched, it dripped.

Well, Father. Were you a builder in stone?
I watched you carry cinder-block
like alphabets, to make walls and walk
instruct us, as if your back
bore Moses' tablets and his rock
willed to shape and final form
in concrete layered shock on shock.

What kind of warfare did we wage?
No omens leaped for either side.
I played with sand; my size what I knew
of weakness, and when I met your wall
there was nothing I could do but dangle feet,
and pluck the imperfect weeds
silently creeping from mortar and dew.

Now you are dead, and if contest is the key
to what your life meant in that silent stride
you made building walls against the slide
and slow corrosion, then I, a stubborn child again,
stand triumphant at your broken side
upon your toys, and take the different view
of earth loose and permanence untied.

Easter

My mother died the same day Jesus did,
give or take two thousand years.
I took her with me when I rose
over Logan, flying at the night.

Easter week Wisconsin smells of cow shit.
Beasts churn the thick black fields,
hairy as roots, dirt-dark, shapeless,
thrusting mud noses among broken stubble.

I trudge-toward my child, I carry my mother
that old refugee, eyes filled with weather,
grass on her breast. Through mock woods
leafless and raw, silent between deaths.

Linda has cancer in her twenty year old liver,
beneath her bosom she swells pregnant with nothing.
Nightly she accepts another plunging lover,
holds us voyeur beside her private grappling.

Morning hens queen their profiles
past my window, appraising the ribbon of light.
Goody two-shoes, lifting narrow feet,
eyes me plodding along the muddy yard.

I came from the ocean, chickie. My soul,
its wrenching, like amino acid
struggling free swarmy with life
wasn't molded from Dane County clay.

Yet beneath quilted yellow fields a woman
asleep trembles, disturbing lands I clambered on,
coaxing to waken. Wide as the county nurse,
wind rattles the kitchen door.

A fingerless sun picks at the kennel chain.
Linda whimpers her dream, her small head
a bruised strawberry spoiling the pillow.
Is it time now to loosen the dogs?

Across the horizon flat farms
square every question. A house,
a barn, a silo, a pasture. House, barn, silo,
pasture. Thrust from the sea we condense

brittle as stranded starfish,
starved as the final dinosaur,
and awash, awash, awash
within our unreckoning wombs.

Next Time Send For Me

Grand-aunts fall like ripened pears,
and old uncles quietly die while we,
away on business, miss the funerals:
Aunt Lillie passed away last week, burst
from her body in the silence of milkweed
escaping a scrawny stem. The answering
service didn't know how to reach you.

The generations reflect, mountains caught
in water. Uncle Spiro, shriveled after-birth,
stares at hands deposed and useless on his
lap. When will he die? Has he died already?
And curled children, decorations on a
store-bought cake, grin from the floor
at the flash-bulb's bidding. Where was I?

I wish you'd called me back across the autumn
leavings to stand on artificial grass and watch
her chocolate box lowered while the old ladies'
last chilled whimpers faded. Some don't remember
who I am—Harry's younger daughter. I don't
remember who died one year ago; I guess
who'll go next, and take her hand.

So I make my way, rank by rank
past squirming babies on the rug
to adolescent with my arm upon my seated
father's shoulder, to occupy the seat
he left; my daughter stands; aunts and uncles
quiver in the thinning chairs, their faces
starched brocades of dun and silver. I'd rather

stagger with each season's repetitious grief
than wake to find the final throne is open
and myself captured queen without time
to decipher among women of my own blood
intricate messages inscribed
pale brown across the pear's cool skin.

Wild Ponies

The day before spring like an old
yellow dog stretched on her side,
the field lay with fur stroked smooth
by northerly winds. Birds whistled
and twitted like pinwheels clipped to
black oak branches, small toys unpacked
from last summer. I hunched up the
flank of the hill among frost heaves
healing like scabs. Mud rusted my boots
but your hair remained golden as Buffalo
Bill's; you were grinning in the fracas of wind.

Overlooking the water we rested on pillows
of sun tossed around by clouds.
Putting my ear to the ground I heard
what robins hear, and with my other
ear your voice recounting how
once you saw a herd of wild ponies.
I plucked an ivory Japanese spoon
left dried on a milkweed stalk
and filled it with wrinkled berries
grown old in the grass; you held
in your palm a straw of wild wheat
and stroking its mane told how the ponies
scattered like seed toward the mountain.

When you left I kept pod
and berries the way one carries off
Kodachromes of places never returned to,
soap from hotels in one-night cities,
or luminous sea-stones and wampum,
knowing beforehand salt
will be lost to the odor of pockets
already paid with indifferent travels. Only
behind your departing back this yellow dog sleeping
twitches and runs out of her dream;
stands to shake dust from a jacket needing
repair, finally pads through the open
door looking for something.

Story Time

The white rabbit runs white fields
leaving black egg-shaped spoor like tadpoles
to swim the sharp snow,
or pellets of rye bread
crumbed to mark Hansel's trail home.
(Birds consumed that precaution,
dropped their incontrovertible message:
There Is No Way Out Of This Forest.)

Someone lied about rabbits,
white only in departing, the tail
a note perched on a dresser. Rabbit is
a brown leather glove, one sock
fallen on the rug, brown
hair of your nut-brown lady. Rabbits
are brown as green grasses of August
displaying jocular victory-sign ears.

The worst winter for a hundred years:
footprints appear at the doorway,
triangular leaps of the hungry who
overplayed summer and the plowed-
under corn. Practical, I hope no starveling
shelters beneath the porch where Tabby
disregarding two thumps from an unlucky
foot will retort, "Rumpelstiltskin!"

But make it back to the thicket,
to the briar patch where no fox can follow.
Read me the part where ice tempered by night
releases to earth a trail, and thaw
scatters white pollen. Rain drives down the seed.
And then will it say in the morning
how Peter and the transfigured
Prince walk homeward on water?

Charles River Goldfish

Everyone knows goldfish in a bowl,
Woolworth pets darting from the convex face
and finger probe of curious love, tomorrow found
death-side up, rotting like orange peel.
Did your mother flush it down the toilet?
Or changing water in the sink, curse
as one olympic swimmer leaped the drain
and like a razor cut his way to freedom?

My fish escaped the year an elbow blistered
boating on the Charles meant peach-pit glands,
penicillin. The arm survived;
denied the boat-house dance, bright with fever
I fantasized pastel scenes, doll embraces.
The inward dream also was begun:
thoughtful measure of the coiled orange heart
waiting in the murk beneath the dock.

Decades later with my sixth or seventh lover
strolling on the Esplanade I glimpse
my fish, light reflected from his flaming gills
throbbing like a poppy on the water.
My goldie wed to yours, to all the daring
five and dime survivors, supple brides
of burning winters. Not ghost,
better than ghost, adapter, avatar.

Recognizing me his mouth smiles and closes
on the soup of urban river, sewer sludge,
sweat off Harvard sculls; his wide body
simple as redemption, with fins open hands.
We dance, we sail, we accept a proffered cigarette
and resting on the guardrail watch bright
stitches embellish the surface-play above the fish,
enlarged, illumined, more pliable than gold.

Moon Shot

Quick before the moon is full
and spills its golden lode
of scanners back upon us let's
beloved you and I enjoy one further
epicycle, rotation on the planetary
floor, I mean let's dance.
The Totem Pole Ball Room
before its demise held this:
globes of turning stars multi-prismed
as an insect's eye; your face light-
shot pink and purple with confetti
as the whirling worked, and as we
waltzed my hand upon your serge
caught dotted-swiss the musical rain.
We danced, we dipped, I thought sixteen
was candy and all there was.

And now the moon has changed,
moon which lit my cheek when first
you kissed me, probing with your tongue
new territory. The moon's an old
dish now; not cheese but dust, not star-
dust but rock decayed and worn by meteors
and boots; everything is known:
the hand upon the latch, the opening door
heard only with the heart, the hard
foot-print no winds ease, then or ever.

Who wants to dance? Let's engineer
a stairway to the stars, and if we meet
descending Jacob's furious angel, wish
him luck; the odds have really changed:
we all wrestle now, and brawny Jacob
who served among naive nomadic tents
was kicked upstairs; he's crossing gibbous
deserts with two hundred bawling kids.

Poem For My Grandchild

I hear my grandson shouting in the street.
He's nine years old.
He's five states eastward
shouting in a different time zone
an hour before I hear his boy's
knife-sharpener voice travel the keen
sunlit space shouting, "Throw the ball! Here!
Here!" For an arm like mine, fifteen hundred
miles is nothing. It's the hour I don't know
how to put a spin on.

My daughter telephones. Conversation goes:
"What does he call you?"
"He calls me 'Mama'. He's adapting quickly."
"Do you give him lots of hugs and kisses?"
"Yes. He wants a bicycle. He needs new shoes already.
He wants the dog to sleep with him. I say
absolutely no. Some nights the dog cries.
A mother must be firm."
"He'll call me 'Nana'. When we visit
in July I'll buy a bike for him."

It’s May, now. Little boys wait
two months before needing a bath;
two months testing the patience of captured
toads; two months teach how the brass-bright
eyes tarnish and fold. Over this boy,
imported grandchild dressed
in language I scarcely know, time bends
to fit my family’s clothes; lengthens legs
for jeans, demands Stride-Rite shoes;
lets out vocabulary for aunts and cousins
whose embraces come in English.

Birth is an arduous season of green
legal papers, forest of a thousand
generations tucked away in fossil caves,
their bones the fuel we burn on.
Courts declare our kinship. I tell
no-one I hear the child calling at his games,
or that in my dreams a white stitched ball
insubstantial as a daylight moon curves
back and forth between us, now his, now mine;
caught in the orbit of this radiant
design it embellishes the hour between us.

BRIGHT SEDIMENT

Bright sediment, rebel leaf
launched on its own gold gallantry,
fish who learned to dwell in fire –I remember the lake
where once I saw God, or what I thought
was god, in a gathering of luminous air
glorifying crowns of trees.
And I recall the trees, enormous
pine that swallowed lightning,
the trunks with fungus extended
in polished shelves, and shimmering birch.

I remember our dirt and gravel road where sharp
November grasses creaked; in May,
wings from waking maples floated. Raspberries
grew on our lawn. Each summer I found
rubies on the ground. Because they pleased me
every year Len gloved against the thorns
to prune and pull the restless brambles.
He was a man whose skin and bones
uttered themselves as rocks and flowers do;
above the gauntlets blue veins on his arms
collected light; it seemed the hair shone
from a source inside him, or me, I hardly knew.

All that is easy. What's harder is
not forgetting what the water thought,
what memory each tree intended to pronounce,
the personal murmur of stone and swirling
sand. That conscious world
that sometimes would unfold to me
each atom of its willful light
opening and shutting like a firefly
or umbrella-star; or better say,
like desire, itself to be what it was,
and only that; and that, its charm and doom.

I had no choice. They took us out by boat.
Beneath the water I saw through an open
window the yellow curtain floating.
A quiet ruin. No one screamed
or called, birds fled and even dogs,
left swimming toward
the diminished hill swam quietly, their eyes
half closed. Len was gone; I don't know
how. I knew of his death when I saw
below the oars alyssum in our yard
close down its blossoms one by one;
and the white gate turned dark, as if
never again was anyone expected.

I came here alone to learn the desert:
dry stones clacking and fierce birds.
I learned to live without rivers, and without
a husband; for a long time I slept
clasping my own hand. When I could see again
I didn't trust it, the light, although
it never lied. It was my own idea of god,
mistaking what was promised. Nothing
was for me; it was themselves they spoke
and when I heard the voice of mesquite
and cactus I finally remembered what the home
lake used to whisper: I am myself.
Not grief, but laws of grief remain eternal.

The following year I journeyed to the ocean.
I wanted to be where sand confronted water,
each heaped on its own side with hills
unsubstantial and heavy. On dunes I found
bitter beach grass, charred stumps from deserted
fires, gutted crab shells. Nothing was strange
but my need: from shale I sorted
pebble from pebble as fishers with nets empty
in separate baskets their harvest of silver and blue;
while at my back the wild plum flourished
and pierced like the cry of a choir.

But I had always known everything bright
darkens; and dark, it loses form:
the shape loosens, colors have no reason.
When we were children we used to ask
where does the flame go when the match
is blown? I supposed it slipped away
to where another candle waited.
And if what I saw was god
I see it still, in this house, keeping
intact the patio, the pillows, the flowers
on the table. And where the sun drifts,
wait things that died and things that will
re-form; at night when the fire is lit
I see how the wood, leaving, shines.

The Room

Windows define the room, not these white
walls. Where one looks from, is where one is:
aloft in light. Black limbs of three-
story trees braid strands of the graying sky.
Squirrels. One heavy crow, stiff-throated jays.
Far below shines the snow-cleaned park with buried
courts and stone walls daubed with legends.
Cross-country skiers wade into trails, children
drag plastic sleds; then stage right enters
a couple hand in hand. She unfurls a blue umbrella
because yes now it rains and two dogs unexpectedly
stand white in the blackening snow.

What one sees from a room is the room's mind,
heart, histories projected. On the sill hyacinth
quivers on tall green legs; clustered blossoms,
too high on their leap, shriveled and frail.
In the shallow bowl the bulbs pebble-ballasted
on a tangle of white string roots went dry.
There's nothing to do but wait out the season.
Why do you play this music, thick tapes of requiems
sung decades ago? On my knees among voices
I watch the dark branches barely higher than where
they jostled when you as a boy didn't know elm from oak,
and although you love them, you still don't know.

What you see from the windows of this room
is yourself believing a house where you always
lived will never be yours, will forever belong
to your father whose cane hangs from the door-knob,
whose portrait hangs on the wall, whose voice
entertains with Irish stories taped on your time
machine when he was eighty; will belong to your
strong-loved mother who recited the rosary and left
indomitably ugly dishes in your cupboards forever.
The filmed glass is yours. The view is yours from
hours you obediently kneeled, and while the Hail
Marys droned listened instead to the patter
of animals looting the attic, and wild crying birds.

Sunlight wakes us, and from your naked back
radiates a warmth like February sun. This is
Day Two. Light refracts from the walls. Ceiling
recedes high above the futon laid on the floor.
Without lifting my head I understand that snow,
renewed in my dreams, washed the city park
clean of sin. Inside this room with your white
rainbow quilt, the empty director's chair, the wide
plank oak floor flat as a raft, only windows
have weight. I am your guest. You took me
to your parents' graves to introduce me.
Over the dead azaleas I stood and said howdoyoudo's until

your father's bright brogue told a molasses flood
tale, when syrup flowed high as the horses' collars
and brave firemen saved thousands from death surely
by pumping hot water into the hoses.
Then perhaps it's a trick of the view, of applauding
the acts of trees. I could write anything here.
I could be you, playing back memories as if
they were mine, become in the moment mine,
because in the white view we form two parts of one
struggle, the sleeping body freckled and curled
on its hip like rock set in the shore-line submerged
and exposed; the waked eye that looks outward tracing
hawk-flight and craters of the daytime moon.

Having brought to bed juice, coffee, the morning
news, it seems easier to stay in this one white
respite from crooked storage closets and stacked
trunks of untouched ironed linens. I think
of my love as a silence I offer, a hand reaching out
to rub your shoulders, motions as old as tide,
the frail interim of water at rest. When we fall
back to sleep with your arm beneath my neck
and my leg beneath your waist in that old lovers'
knot of incalculable comfort light on the branches
has moved like a key in a lock.
By late afternoon the park turns blue; the sky
like a great stone rolled to the mouth of some
new tomb seals access to the sledding hill.
Children, run home. The nuns of remembrance
return to tidy their book and chalk rooms;
their fierce rules return with them like shadows;
they stiffen their wimpled wings, crying to us who are childless
that we stay after school their captives forever.

The Third Day, planned and determined for duty,
surprises us with yet another storm, cutting off
the vista with fine fierce snow. Now truly we know
this room hides among other rooms endlessly
maddened with unpacked boxes, a wind-up victrola,
saved Irish coins, bottles of never-used glycerin
pills for the heart. I am assigned to clear cooking
space, lift out dry pots, replace utensils become
untouched antiques. From the parlor I hear you
shift cartons of obligations, thud dry newspapers
into the trash. When you call me to see the gold time-
piece stretched on its chain like a small untouched
hand I kiss your whitening hair and the grief
of your smile, and while you put your father's
house in order one more time I set chairs around
the table; tomorrow we invite the young neighbors over.

The telephone rings, unobtrusively as Sunday
bells in the distant church whose green cross-capped
spire triangles the luminous snow.
We are connected. In each room lamps obediently
brighten to a touch, heat stirs old dust before
the vacuum carries it away, spring cleaning.
While you speak on the phone the hose
inhales cobwebs lacing the cornice;
a dare pulls down your mother's instructive curtains.
I want to hang in the windows fern, gaudy fuchsia,
begonias with darting tongues. Violets flower
in every season. I wait to tell you their colors
while the waked furniture of your childhood
moves stiffly from one room to another finding
a level floor, a use, the surprise of its newer grace.

Beavers Have Called

Beavers have called rain
down from the fretting creek
onto the basin where broken-
tooth tree stumps go hungry.
Their dam takes in its arm
cottonwood and maple; cane
swoons in dark Jordan waters
awaiting a long immersion.

I never aspired
to change the shape of a garden,
summon fish, make waves, raise islands
but wouldn't it be easy
playing Blessed Lady of Landscapes
if I could redeem fallen branches,
if I could breathe smoke from this river's candles.

ALTERNATIVES

I once had a lover, Eugene,
who one day revealed to his wife
each of his theories of drama, dance, myth,
astrology, politics, the Pentateuch
until nothing remained unmentioned.
Eugene calmly declared,
I go to my room to die.

I bear my version of the Midas curse:
everything I touch turns to fiction.
Eugene, I never meant to lie.
But had you understood
the art of alternatives
you too would still be alive.

PART TWO

Letting The Seasons

THE WATCH-MAKER

The watch-maker's name was Jacquet-Droz.
When he tired designing delicate Swiss clocks
on his home slope of the Jura where time
doesn't matter he made people. Two were boys
who wrote their names, made sketches
of a dog (mon toutou), counted ten. Neat
from birth they wore white ruches at their necks,
never chewed their graphite pencils.

The other was a girl. Seventeen perhaps,
with cogs and cams hidden in her palms,
behind her perfumed ears, between her breasts.
One hardly knew, from how she smiled
and played the organ without rewinding,
how small her thoughts. Jacquet-Droz
named her Marianne, his dead wife's name,
and took her on triumphal European tours
where she breathed with bellows and curtsied
to applauding princes. He loved her, I suppose,
the porcelain and the honey-colored curls.
He sold her to a French firm in Madrid
when revolution stopped the luxury trades,
and wandered back to Switzerland. In the serious
mountains he settled down and made a clock
so fine it measured centuries between two
snowflakes falling against his brass-locked door.

Left Child

(after the Pied Piper of Hamelin)

Grave with surprise the child emerged
from the belly of the mountain
when the voices and failing tune
died behind curtains of stone.
Alone with his slow lame foot he
nudged lambs at their casual graze
for something to answer. Their metal bells
opened alarm as they fled away.

Now he must descend empty paths
to town halting at each gate to explain
how both rats and children were gone,
and flocks to the faint hill strayed
with tiny chimes close even those
distant pied musical caves.

Overpass

Under Muddy River overpass pigeons doze,
and a gaunt man grown fat with news
cunningly wrapped around his torso
beneath a sweater, and inside his shoes.

Newborn birds gape from their buttress nest:
a brackish mess of twigs raggedly thrust
between steel supports. The joists
hollow their straw thin chirps.

Damp shadows. Curled on his side the man
in fetal nightmare, around his mouth brown
crust of blood coughed, swallowed, and coughed
like a prior life refusing to stay down.

Muddy River fondles evil thoughts
like a neglected fortune teller, waits
in her cellar brewing omens. The man snores,
shallows in his skull purple blots.

The pigeon sergeant stays awake, bad
white cop wearing chevrons. He watches hard
the vibration of crossing trucks, human dying,
river dark with malevolent leaves unread.

RIVER

The net of his eye caught
nothing; his black hand stiffened grasping
starvation. Trash-pickers of holy salvage
saved this infant raccoon, still breathing.

Demanding life they heated his belly,
chafed his ribs like Aladdin's lamp.
The scarlet cave of his mouth gaped:
the tabernacle whose Laws were stolen.

He abandoned his cradled skull while
sugar-milk prayers knocked at his jaw;
curled on the rigid sky
a crescent moon was stubbornly waning.

They buried the corpse ceremoniously
among forsythia, fern, lilac. Finders-
keepers, insist he yield one
dark inch of compliant blossom.

His Mother

Thomas tells me how his mother broke
both his legs with a baseball bat,
fractured his clavicle, beat him
senseless til cops came seeking
his screams found him beneath the bed
bleeding.

None of this is true.
Now Thomas avoids me
like a corner he peed in, hides
in a book pretending he's reading.
Secretly I watch him for hints of wreckage,
broken veins leaking pulses,
broken knee-caps shouting through
his skin. I want to glimpse
his mother's fingerprints along his jaw,
her desperate grip, her shrill
I never touched you why do you hate me.

Generation Gap

Her husband died; his departure
an abdication by the czar
reveals Gloria's hungry ribs.

Their daughter drives a cab, her eyes gray sieves.
Gloria, former Jewish mother,
hawks radical issues of The Newsmart,

peddles outrage from a pushcart
like her hopeful father
once cried knives and scissors

candelabra, small tin mirrors.

The Dance

Michelle from another universe
dances like a broken star,
her hair in flakes narrow as night,
her black eyes the color of absence.

Michelle pirouettes, a wind-up doll.
Tunes of home, fledglings lost,
fall in the bramble of her smile,
the weighted branch of her throat quivers.

Lifting my deaf inflexible feet
over acres of public floor I approach her;
my sane hands capture her shoulders.
For a moment a foreign music holds

us posed in a paralyzed waltz.

Eden's Sparrow

(for Eden Wallace, November, 1982)

Eden holds in her hand a fallen sparrow
lifted from the dashed glass and concrete
patio where it contemplated early autumn.
With long fingers she caresses the hollow
between its wings. The bird weighs motionless
gold in her palm, leaves trembling
and terror to me.

Do what? Find somewhere its nest
lined perhaps with brambles gleaned
from a hairbrush on a mirrored tray,
or with single moon-coiled threads of pink
and pansy, stolen from floating summer
dresses on a clothesline, and carried
to that nest imagined in a distant garden.
Eden croons, her hair above the muted bird
swinging as girls will swing their hair
to summon lovers.

Later when I ask what happened to the bird
she says, "It flew away." Then, over her
shoulder, "A nice experience." The trees nearby
ripple with sparrows brown as breakfast
toast, with salad song. Eden saunters
on another errand, her dark hair moving
like the door to a further room;
here, no bird is missing.

Lullaby

Sleep, children, sleep,
stretched in sleeping bags
across an unused playroom floor,
head and arms tumbled into dawn.
May no intruder wake you, far from home.

Sleep, children, while the world
turns you like the season's
fallen fruit, with faces
sad and old and never grown;
sleep, children, who have no other home.

You arrive with New Year's Day.
Bedrolls, backpacks, straps
tangle in your hair and close your eyes;
denim pilgrims come on foot alone
from urgent friends: they have no home.

Sleep, children. I have lived
in this one house longer than the years
you've been alive; I never rode
two hundred miles from home.
My babies born here grew and now are gone

as meant to go. Send me word:
Christmas greetings, postal cards, from
Oregon, Canterbury, Rome. We learn
no more of questing than we have always known.
Sleep, children, sleep, far from home.

Wind From The South

A moist wind blows from the south.
She looks like magnolia, glitters like
silver. At the window he senses coming
the bifurcation, the path of air
through grass. Her skin is a field
of blossoms absorbed in reflection. He wishes
to take her the way a pebble is taken by the sea.

And this is the braid of their lives: that
he will place on her breast his firm hand,
waking her when the shower's whisper
joins their bed like another lover.
Before morning, he knows, the flowers
arranged on the table will forget their original
language, and stars coiled behind clouds
will have drowned in their own spiral rain.

That her instep is his requirement, lilac
veins mapping her ankles, heavy
hills of her flesh. He wants to plant himself
like cypress, feeling her uterus lift
and fall in the lake of his passion.
This would be, he thinks, re-enactment
of land appearing on the face of the waters.

He does not, watching her image undress
in distant grace on the glass, recall creating
his children, twins destined to birth when
long ago, lounging naked Sunday in bed
feeding each other fruit, he for the first
time allowed his fingers to wonder
at the formal light tracing her spine,
at the color of new juice on her mouth.

Two-Faced Woman

The hunchback waitress-and-cook
must sell behind her thin shoulders
an extra breast bold with bone nipple.
Arms nimble, she dips with the menus
courting the hand that will cup her
whispering, "Janus of sunset and dawn,
of loveliness coming and going,
show me your other face." At a table
one man waits, shut inside band aid eyelids,
keeps his crumpled lips hidden,
sweats out his recognition.
Then carefully wipes with a napkin
his already dry chin, leaves a tip.
She's already forgotten she loved him.

Trash-Picker

The Wednesday woman comes to scavenge trash
behind buildings in the parking lot
where refuse makes castles for princess rats.
She pushes a pram filled with cast-off
clothing and dolls, with babies perhaps;
carefully chooses from plastic bags
a chair cushion, broken comb, tin cookie box.
The backs of her knees map mountains
above her withered brown socks.

Woman, get away from here; tenants
with their hundred open eyes are staring.
Long hands will rush to take from you
your peacock throne, your waving hair,
the sweet feast cakes you and your darlings share.

Winter Comes For Marcia

Crows litter the fields with old notions,
broken dishes, lost children. The wind somewhere
beseeches. Behind a plasterboard sky no secrets:
the king rails at the neighborhood witch
who enchanted his daughter. The nearest city
means a sixty-mile drive on a half-filled tank.

Seedpods dry empty as eggs when the sharp
fox departs. Marcia bakes bread all day. Her little
boy digs in the yard. He wants to see what's
revealed to blind worms underground. For shovel
he plies a geranium, and wears a round red
geranium for hat. It warms his earthen hair.

The narrow cement walk squeezes her;
squelching through mud can't redeem her. Am I
the last rag linked to the poplar. She no
longer hopes to hear robins chip the wood
sides of her buried efforts. She stores
black loaves in her boneless cupboards.

On the solstice Marcia caresses the rim
of a cup like skin on the back of a lover,
recalling by touch words he had spoken.
When she puts down the cup she remembers
words he didn't say. Fish with no gifts
frost the windows. A draft sets the lamp swimming.

A new moon has been carried onstage, brief
as a Chinese dragon, rice-paper thin. Steeples
and shooting stars clang, and the peremptory south-bound
train. Marcia's little boy is asleep but Marcia
keeps reading. On her castle door stretch briars
vast as black cats in the darkness whose prince is coming.

How Dame Julian Named The Multitudes

Some designations she knew: a congregation
of people, a host of men; and in her natural
green-struck church she knew beyond a doubt
that God creating man and wife, and creatures
two by two, commanded all to multiply.
Then smiled and took a Sunday nap. And now
how? Such multitudes, such aggregates appeared
unnamed from that relentless obedience to breed.

Therefore she undertook, both duty and her sin
of pride to choose the labels destined, so she
dreamed, to last a thousand generations. From
Norwich, as she looked upon a herd of harts,
and then of cranes and wrens,
her imagination leaped. A siege of herons, she cried
as they polished bitter wings along the marshes.
And when dusk gathered, she whispered: a watch
of nightingales, all is well. A flight of doves
was how she called the pale birds touching
like thoughtful hands the grassless scratch
of yard; but when on royal lawns among the lime
trees peacocks fanned their drumming colors
her bosom swelled beneath the ironed gray restraint;
she saw, she thought of yeomen gone with banners,
and declared, a muster.

And so she waxed in pride, and named a pride of lions,
a clattering of choughs, a skulk of foxes who
robbed the hens and left red upon the stones their consort
rooster cruelly murdered. She deduced a slew of bears
when shepherds fled chattering without their lambs;
a gaggle of geese garbled song in the kitchen yard.
But she was growing old, that insatiable Lady,
and in fear cried fie upon a pontificate of prelates
who kept her from her yearning rounds among the
novices, sweet chicks scarcely in their menstrual
blood who blushed and gladdened when this Mother
touched their peach-dew cheeks. How could they know,
those innocents, that in her dreams Dame Julian
midnightly joined the drunkenship of cobblers,
and frolicked lewdly sucking fingers and toes
while stroking their buttocks, until at dawn
she woke from dream to prayer, and feared the empty
jug and feared her palsied hand. As timely she
increased in age and dissolution, the Dame clutched
her gown about her neck and stared, whispering,
an abominable sight of monkeys, Lord; let me see more.

VILLANELLE: FOR BOSTON'S MOUNTED POLICEWOMAN

Her burnished mount descends the skipping stair
When noonday flaunts a golden banner sun.
Amber stallions dance toward Copley Square.

Fountains ravish light upon the air.
Through skeins of rainbow stretched and spun
Her burnished mount descends the skipping stair.

At the mayor's bandstand trombones flare
But far off where the hurdy-gurdy melody's begun
Amber stallions dance toward Copley Square.

Matrons, motionless with arms and bosoms bare
Free glitter-children. Say in whose imagination
Her burnished mount descends the skipping stair

Among jeweled lovers lustrous on the grass, the rare
Flesh whose dream, whose musical configuration
Amber stallions dance. Toward Copley Square

Magic makers hasten when hoof on brick unaware
strikes the rim of time. Trembling on this crystal fabrication
Her burnished mount descends the skipping stair;
Amber stallions dance toward Copley Square.

FATHER SIMON

Beneath his cassock hairless thighs
rub like rumors when he walks.
Perennial rashes bloom with injunctions
not to scratch. His hands contain
each other; one released for grasping
platitudes leaves the other a child
without a father. A holy man, he wears
his washed face open so anyone can tell
he snacks chocolate bars close to supper.
When children come to make confession
he frets, "God knows everything we do."
The kids, released to asphalt business
run through puddles and ignore
threats their mop-worn mothers utter.
Only Father Simon, listening from the high
vestry window believes every truthful scold
and undertakes to suffer.

The Story Of Noah

Noah, outside at six every morning,
whanging away, waking the neighbors,
ignored blue weather and fended
rude comments; he knew what he needed,
he worked the wood.

The design was decreed: three hundred
cubits three stories high; in his mind
giraffes took hay from the rafters;
moles and rodents sheltered in corners,
snakes in the beams, birds in the cornice.
Yes, a window above and a door in the side.

He began with the keel. A great golden
cage captured the sky as he lay down the ribs.
Loafers looked into the heart of the
matter: Noah with shoulders of gopher wood
shavings bent his beard to the adz,
a week left to labor.

While the weather stayed sunny
he pegged the rough planks, section
by section enclosing his timber,
and finally pitch sealed in those secrets
neighbors had known once
but lately forgotten.

So Noah captained his great trembling
bowl filled with beasts and their mates
and fowl and their droppings. Feathers
and odors and fur filled his nostrils;
his wife and sons and daughters-in-law
stood on the deck waving and weeping.

What held them afloat while water above
scrubbed loose their feelings,
and flood below erased all their friends?
They sailed here to here on a dark ten-month
journey and woke on a mountain
crowning the world.

Then Noah stepped down from the door
on the side, and felt with his foot
the Ararat soil. In his hand
rolled some seeds. At his back three sons
waited. He was six hundred years old,
all he owned was a rainbow.

Frost

Grasshoppers die in the cold,
two-inch hooded widows, folded
refugees next to the road. Too weary
to move; flung in convulsions of grief
from wagon-high grass, sprawled on their backs,
yellow shins and coarse thighs broken wide.

The sky stays blue no matter who dies,
or who weeps on her gravel-pocked knees,
as did old derelict Fran on shocked city
streets when thugs grabbed her shopping
bag leaking bloomers and socks,
doomed rain-hat with chin strap lost,
stale caraway rolls. All I own,
grasshoppers cry, but the shoes on my
feet and the frost on my bones.

Isidore Age Ninety

Isidore's eyelids are too weary to admit the world;
at ninety dust collects behind his lenses on his
lashes, and finds the collar of his rusted coat.

Everywhere he goes he goes alone; his friends
hide breathless while he steers the perilous streets,
last ghost upright in the line for judgment.

Isidore writes verses, and strives to eke
from every half-blind word the essence of his quarrel
with God, who like the landlord raises rents

but never makes a substantive improvement. God
over Isidore's apartment grows guilty when the pestering
intensifies, and sifts upon the wedge of hair

of His persistent tenant blessings fine as
falling plaster. Daily Isidore becomes more white
and filmy; air fits about him like an alabaster box.

Isidore wants God to share with him His Ultimate Idea
but God who long ago let slip to Isidore all there is
to know, only answers, "I already told you," and waits

for Isidore to get tired, and go.

PART THREE

Letting The Seasons

LETTING THE SEASONS

First it's snowing. Then it's raining. Little
green things jump out of the ground.
Then leaves turn yellow and fall. Soon it snows.
During that time you might do a birth or death,
fight with a friend, visit on Christmas Eve quiet
Aunt Ruth. At no time will you squat on the window
sill like a cat and watch birds bathe in the puddle
on the rooftop below you, nor eat a fallen begonia
flower, nor turn the radio knob with your toes.

In no time will you watch weathers turn sideways,
and slide hand-over-face across you sun or rain,
while you turn pages of old journals and eat
squat chocolates from a heart-shaped box:
the cat on the sill twitches her tail at birds
who bathe like old ladies at Tampa their fallen
bosoms and yellow bunion-capped toes.

During this time, the smooth turn of seasons,
you will take from closets changes of coats,
put in or out boots and gear, switch hats for New
Year and Easter and never go visit Aunt Ruth, because
one seasonal day she died quiet as a cat sunned to
sleep in a window, and when her daughter dared open
the stash of precious journals all Aunt Ruth had written
was whether it rained or snowed, for sixty years,
for sixty years, and common and Latin names
of birds flown past her various windows.

The Seagull

this seagull is not lost
he takes the city for sea
skims the surface of air
fishes from picnics in the park.

white bird, white as a thought
in a blue eye: all things
are the same - heaving streets
people tossing in the sun

two deaf girls
flexing their starfish hands.

THE SEA SERPENT

The night the serpent died tidal waves
struck Pakistan; Chile shook with revolution;
bombs enlivened downtown Gloucester.
Who could have known which moment gates
beneath the earth opened to disgorge
slime and fish, crabby beasts,
whelks, eels, and fairy princes; or that
with them came the serpent thrust from home.

Like a sad-eyed horse he roamed the ocean
grazing algae and sea-lettuce; with ancient
psalms he sundered schools of fish, broke
the heart of continents. Seemingly
he had no wound or blemish,
until he folded wasted wings, and perished.

No one knew why. Oceanographers arrived
to find his carcass vandalized and
his jawbone stolen; curious onlookers
came to kick his hide, carve peace
symbols and initials. Scientists
classified his fins and chambered heart, left
desecrated flesh for slugs and gulls,
went to type reports.

The third day on the sand perfected ruin.
Sun-bright birds wrung free, leaving hermit
crabs to polish white the vaulting of his ribs.
Whispering, at dusk tides approached his skull
and deftly entered to arrange among the rubble
block and chain. And raised the marble.

October First

This the season for splitting,
for spilling seed and fruit;
leaves leap from stems, horse chestnut
crack their prickly hedgehog backs,
acorns swell, apples tumble from the trees.

Rain-fall, four days and nights;
squelching past a florist shop
I spot a bunch of tight-assed yellow roses
warming their stems;
march in, hustle them into

Sudden brisk recruitment of northeast wind
parading the chosen clouds away.
The sky snaps open like a Chinese fortune cookie.
Out falls the -what's it say- rice paper
sun?

Clocks

On Tuesday the alarm clock released its breath
and snapped a corset string. Time bulged gaily
fore and aft.
Thursday the electric clock collapsed,
lying on the kitchen wall, hands folded.

Outraged I uncased its corpse,
undid its fasteners, and in the frail
motor of its universe I slid my tiny hammer. Zap.
Capped the wires, fixed the facing.
Hung the wall on its back like a crucifix and watched
tomorrow approach
while I fasted on a wooden kitchen chair,
blinking thorns from my eyes. Saturday
I went to bed. The clock stopped.

On Monday time resumed.
But now the clocks rested in the trash, obliged
to no-one, fed on carrot tops and tins.
I heard them chomping in the bag slung
from the janitor's back, as his feet descended
the rhythmic stairs.

Lights

When I was a kid lights never came on.
We had a War. Dumb Benjie with his thatch
in a basin labeled Warden poked our windows
when the blackout curtains leaked.
Light! cried Benjie, Light!
as if light were sodomy, candles flickering
goats who admired him. Citizen decorators
blackened the State House dome like a coal chute.

Now I notice how twin lights
across this placid street at dusk
enhance my neighbor at his casement
advertising jockey shorts.
Their yellow beams cut tenement roofs
and paste them on the faded paper sky.
Dumb Benjie is unemployed. His wife
soaks her bunions in the helmet, uses his nightstick
to converse with stray dogs.

River Source

The river stretches in its lair; one snow,
one stone-throw more, makes winter spill
off its lap: a mess of last October's leaves,
ooze-encrusted weeds and logs,
caught images of bank-bound trees.

Winds awake. Wood thrush call,
ducks wingskim across the stirring water.
The hide sloughs loose, the purple spine
shines in shed silver scales. It moves,
it moves, lustful and huge,
while the sky rains
blue like berries from a pail.

River raise your perilous head,
your wet eye cuts the sun to gems.

Whale Watch

The sun at the center of motion
stirs the winnowing wings
of angels astride the Atlantic
whose pinions of light shift like
milkweed or snow on the surface.

Their fingers make wonder of welter:
jellyfish, sea-grass, sea white
prow of the ship slicing water;
blindly we grope at the railing
and then someone calls, out there

the wake of migrating whales
steadily moving before us
in shapes that skip like mountains.
The bull lifts up his head
streaming a banner over the column;

they lift up their tails like gates.

Summer Solstice

Summer starts 12:23. The reminder
reaches me by radio at noon while I'm
still in the car driving toward
the official place. I slip on dark
glasses to be ready, and through the
windshield watch clouds white as starter
signals tremble on their stems.

12:20 I'm parked and sitting
on a bench where the view is best.
The sun is there, alright, a stalled
marathoner half-way up a slope.
I can feel in the heat he gives off
an imminent decision whether to quit.
Blisters on both heels, one thigh trembles.

A red balloon anchored by string bobs
overhead; I flourish a tiny American
flag on a gilded stick. Every second
counts now: another hill, a curve,
a loose dog tripping runners.
This is the longest day, the ache,
the fame when the timer clicks
his thumb: 12:23. The sun moves;
or if you know it doesn't move for whom
do you stand in a public square
yelling and waving a piece of striped paper?

Cutting The Trees

This dead pine refuses to fall.
Even when we cut its feet
it stands, or hangs
by the hair, from other trees.

And we, we push and rope,
making thunder and bolts
of breaking branches, prizing
the corpse from reluctant arms.

Afterwards I straddle the silence,
hold in my hand heart
reeking of resin, drawn in the waving
circles of a very old story.

We knew all along you were dead.
Or not dead. Which did we know?
That transformations go hard even for trees,
wrenched out of your body into the sun.

This Country

Dawn horizon: sun and moon have
changed places. Ahead on the empty clay
road a man and a woman embracing, knee
to knee in drawstring trousers: hers
turquoise, his pale green. Both wear
faded green blouses with collars.
They are wrapped in a long cashmere shawl;
he, draped as if in a toga, holds her
against his bosom; I see they are kissing.

The next morning I top the same hill:
they remain veiled in her soft
emerald shawl. The third morning
the sky seems frail but the shawl
does not move although mist
shifts on the lake and trees waver.
So I wonder if their kiss is a feature
of this country, like sycamores
or fields of ragged daisies.

The Great Escape

I loved it when the cows escaped
hell-bent for Harry's yard while Harry
on his lawn¬-mower buzzed behind
brandishing his golf-cap and shouting
go home go home!
dogs barked.
birds jeered
Mrs. Harry in the door
shrieked for her azaleas
but the cows plump ladies on the loose
tossed bonnets and bundles every
which-way and disappeared behind
the house reappearing round the other
side like cops and robbers
with Harry featured
as the dumbest cop he didn't even
have a whistle. By now these broad-
beamed bandits were
ambling genteelly toward the local
ice cream parlor
with neatly tied tails
innocent reticules abulge
with milk, motherhood, the peace
of Christ I loved it
when Harry clicked
off his motor and put on his hat.

Thaw

Ice-melt, snow-melt, low
fields' flood, river-spread:

the trees are standing in water.
Water is getting their shoes

wet like old gentlemen curbside
humbled by puddles

too wide to leap,
no sign of a cab, and cars

lifting spray onto trousers
and coat front, splashing like

sickness. These trees were strong
men. I want to think of my father

white as birch when the pain
struck, my father whom hating

I love as he died: pity
the trees

caught in the first flush of spring
with cold water rising

Crossing The Field

We're crossing a field again. It's the same
time of year: nothing green, everything
wishing to be. You are indistinguishable
from unopened leaves. Beneath your skin
swim glees of transparent fish.

Expanding sun overlays shaded
cornfields. Gold bones of last year's harvest
wake ready for burial. It remains cold,
the ground sustains us where naked
stems interlace in a woven basket.

We run; or perhaps you're floating,
an unmoored seine in the river. I follow
smiling as in my photos. Willows once more are
gilding; the gray partridge hurtles
from hiding; this happens each year.

Last spring we went south, the soil was ruddy
and potters made vases for flowers;
women hung cheese in the yards. Once I saw
in a red jar figs black as the hair of a
mandarin's lady; the jar curved like a womb.

Here in the north light differs. Two trees
on a slope construe forests, while sky
stands vertical, innocent, everywhere. This
exists as before. Discarded feathers of swans
brush our dual image onto the millpond

you never pause for. Without motion the field
strokes my ankles. Now nothing moves but the meadow
lark's flute played in the painted straw.
You must wait to help an old woman
climb over a fence. She carries eggs in a kerchief.

MORNING

Mist walks on water like a crowd
of Christs, underweight and weary,
wrapped in twisted robes.
There really is a cock that cries in the narrow
run where white hens bob, small tossing
boats. A woman in scarlet poncho and knee-high
yellow boots shoves barnward the last
cow recalcitrantly mowing clover, sails feed to the chickens.
In the distance a dog coughs.
Horses with dark sloping shoulders
loom in the lower meadow; the woman—
her shrouded form—pauses. The colors
of her gear pierce the fog, or the momentary
way she faces the lake
holding her empty pail.

Flowers Have

flowers have escaped
their duties, have fled
from hospital corridors, made secret
way by freight
elevators down to the streets;
flowers have abandoned
the dead in mahogany frames; they have
eloped without the bride; flowers
have neglected aunts and elderly
mothers, disappeared during Sunday dinners;
flowers growing dim on altars
have recanted and become unbelievers.
two miles south of town
they have occupied an alderman's orchard.
they are unfolding purple slogans.
they are leafleting certain pink trees.

Chakrata Crossing

Sky more impeccable than Mary's mantle,
than the blue skin of Rama watching
himself weightless created, whispering how
this petal becomes, this petal stays,
this petal fades. Sculpted on delicate
mobiles of vines golden leaves
circle the pond. Their flatness taps
to the faint wind a musical clanking.

The seer, legless blossom of white
silk, sings om on Full Moon, requesting
the blessings of masters. Ten thousand
hymns of the Vedas cross his butterfly
hands; he sprinkles four corners of earth
captured by cord linked with silver and coral.
At our feet hiss two guardian swans; the bridge
trembles under tented blue fabric.

"Senses look outward, roots of strong trees
turn within. Seek treasure inside the earth"
dust we stir among bone-gaunt cows,
children with faces of dancers. He closes
his eyes. Four months in this village taught him
to imbibe sleep effortlessly, to join reality
effortlessly; as dawn won't cry out announcing
he finds the pathway in silence.

Mary, for me plead with the mountains
raised from this plain like hammers of random
destruction; translate the pallid brown
grass in the mouth of omnivorous winds.
Help me decipher our journey homeward
among things terrible in thingness; quiet
the mystery of their suffering, hush our weeping
god riddling their lives.

ST. PAUL'S, DESTROYED BY FIRE

This church, roof gone,
offers to time's devotions
rose glass,
buttress, plank door. Heart-dried and burned
it keeps to its builder.
Where are the spirits, saints, angels?
Where ladies in velveteen hats,
pale priests, choir boys with candles?
The entrance fills with dark sod,
cracks in the wall with bird nests.

Only shape remains. Perhaps this is faith at last,
what we sought, what we stayed for—
rock suggesting parameters,
empty except for intention.

The Violinist At Tampa Bay

Wind arrives off the bay and waves
stand stiff as timber. One-legged ducks
napping under purple thunder and scarlet
shade fly to cover. Shoved
to the wall wrappers, bottles, frothing
decay, a black dog's corpse; Then hot
rain hits; palms riff like mad violinists.

She keeps her fiddle boiling on the stove,
a mulligan stew of sound, potatoes,
handfuls of nubby carrots. Before the open
window she stirs her sonorous pot while
the gale stirs, and the sad dog
bumps the dock. When the rain quits
she plays with iron finger-tips
another prelude for the flooded street,

a new world sound, aglow with light like
the stove's electric eye, the night bulb
near the bed, digital time; she is
gathering power when the viking sun
broaches the morning water, and she takes
its measure, saluting with high brilliant song
tall men who stand at the prow straining to hear.

Vertical Landscape At Tampa Bay

Topmost: stars, round fringed flowers on a tulip
tree, lemon pale. This the tree whose trunk
is night, whose days are foliage
blue on the underside, cool, and veined.

Beneath the planets luminous aircraft swarm
yellow-striped, blue-striped, flagged and numbered.
Painting planes she thinks of dogs locked in yards,
the house cat gazing from a kitchen window.
Yet includes in white a rainbow-shaped trail.

Below the airplanes she creates
an arctic. No eskimo, no polar bear, no reindeer
track her horizontal heaps of snow because
here and here a hole appears insinuating
fields of green: a fifth dimension for her two.

On the Tampa side of clouds today
there are no clouds. Sky so remote
scalds the glance. Several heavy pelicans
plow air; nimble gulls with one
eye on the water search for pennies. She
keeps her nose five feet above the ground,
searches odors of mending salt;

on the bay depicts watermelon boats. Tarpon
flare and fall. Such fish require
a pigment of planes, brighter than careless
daubed water. Gulls wear black bonnets over
white angel robes, plunge down like knives.
Fish jump out and birds dive in: two black
women belly-up on the wall with long
nets capture blue crabs for their buckets,
a vertical game.

Under the water fish turn like aging
women before mirrors. A ray floats on hawk-
fingered wings. Sea-grass curls and shadows
the land beneath clouds: rock bottom. In simple
letters she prints THE LEAP STARTS HERE.

The bay's mosaic floor is cracked. The rooted
tulip tree burst an ochre band along the lower
frame. Although no darkness gathers, from somewhere
the slow and fructifying rain her brush demands
ascends. Arrows indicate it's raining
upward toward the stars.

Meeting The Stones

Seeking the company of stones I
pick up pebbles loitering on county dirt
roads: ruffian thumbs of opposable gravel,
crooked hands that dip in my pockets.
Pallid or lean, pudgy or veined,
they are quicker than white-faced cattle
stiff-legged at farmyard fences;
surviving pressures has made them supple.

They invite me to the house of the sun
where dust coats their throats like honey,
and starlings do the flying for them.
I have met rocks among them: a fist
cramped around leaves of blunt summer
and indolent crickets; chunk of dark
muscle engorged with iron; an obdurate
boulder who grips the blue planet
and won't be displaced: I build
my church upon them.

My THINGS

In my house live congenial things:
Ice cream maker, popcorn maker, red china bowl;
born intact from porcelain or maple or chrome
they try adjusting my home-made
face in their own: upside down and
shaped like a pear in a spoon.

I like things, I'm not embarrassed to own.
I neglect them, as I do my sun and my moon.
I leave my fuschia to bloom itself purple;
my books roam across tables, my
dust-pan sulks with my broom. I possess most
what I let alone.
Yet they know when I return
from a trip I'm glad they expected me home.
Make no mistake—
I don't yearn to embrace
each candelabrum.
But occasionally I might kiss a flower. Once
I did kiss a banister. It looked so noble and firm
it reminded me of my husband supporting my arm.

About the Author

Nancy Davies has resided in Oaxaca since 1999. She's the author of personal commentaries dealing with the Oaxaca uprising of 2006. They were published on www.narconews.com and partially collected in book form as The People Decide. Other commentaries by Nancy Davies appeared on http://upsidedownworld.org, from 2008 until 2010.

In her past life Davies' poetry appeared in small and literary magazines. Her previously unpublished works, including poems, novels, essays, and vignettes will be progressively available on http://www.nmsdavies.com, her "writer's selfie."

www.ingramcontent.com/pod-product-compliance
Lightning Source LLC
Chambersburg PA
CBHW071821020426
42331CB00007B/1579

* 9 7 8 0 6 9 2 0 6 8 1 4 4 *